W9-CBE-371

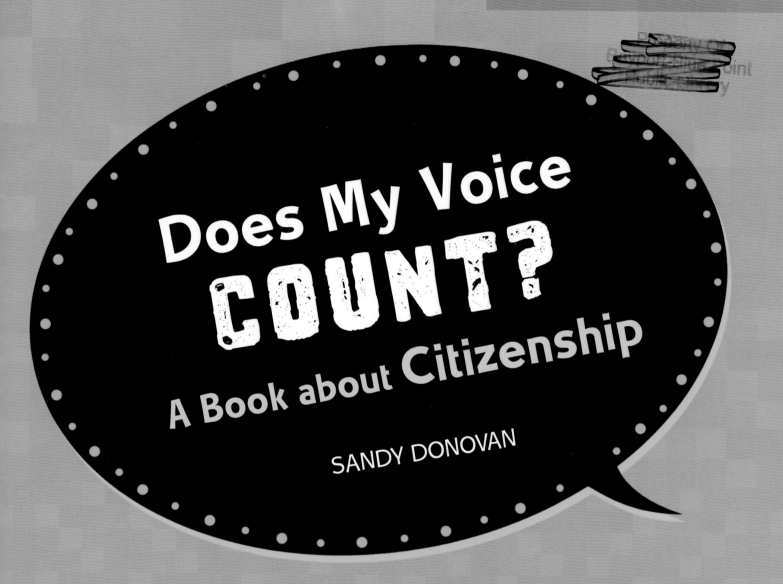

Does My Voice COUNT?

A Book about Citizenship

SANDY DONOVAN

Lerner Publications Company • Minneapolis

Lerner Publications Company
A division of Lerner Publishing Group, Inc.
241 First Avenue North
Minneapolis, MN 55401 USA

For reading levels and more information, look up this title
at www.lernerbooks.com.

Library of Congress Cataloging-in-Publication Data

Does my voice count? : a book about citizenship / by Sandy Donovan.
        pages   cm. — (Show your character)
     Includes index.
     ISBN 978-1-4677-1366-5 (lib. bdg. : alk. paper)
     ISBN 978-1-4677-2522-4 (eBook)
     1. Citizenship—Juvenile literature. 2. Moral education—Juvenile
literature. I. Title.
     JF801.D666 2014
     323.6—dc23   2013019161

Manufactured in the United States of America
1 – MG – 12/31/13

TABLE OF CONTENTS

Do you know what it means to be a good citizen? It means to be a good member of a community. That community might be your country. It might be your school. Or it might be your neighborhood.

There are lots of ways to **make a difference in your community**. You can set a good example at school. You can be a good neighbor. You can listen to adults. You can also volunteer. You can help protect our planet. And you can make your voice heard through your words and actions.

How do you do these things? The following questions and answers will help show you how to be a good citizen!

My mom's friend is running for mayor. My mom is going to vote for her. I'm not old enough to vote. But I want to help too!

HOW CAN I GET INVOLVED IN AN ELECTION?

You may not be able to vote. But there are lots of ways to help. Ask your mom what you can do. Maybe you can pass out flyers or make phone calls. Maybe you can go door-to-door.

Tell others about the people running in the election. Tell them why you want to help your mom's friend. You can also remind people to vote.

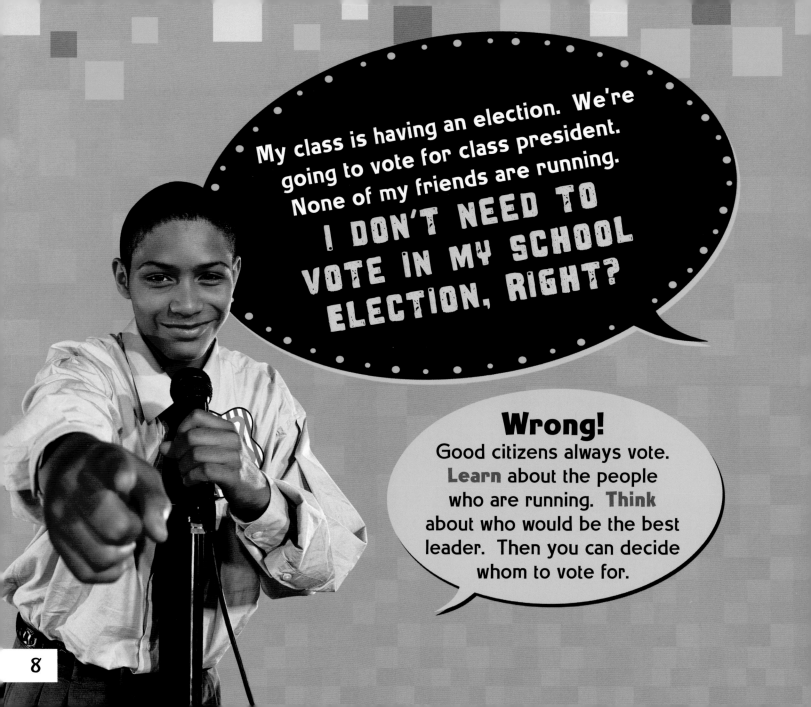

My class is having an election. We're going to vote for class president. None of my friends are running. I DON'T NEED TO VOTE IN MY SCHOOL ELECTION, RIGHT?

Wrong!
Good citizens always vote. **Learn** about the people who are running. **Think** about who would be the best leader. Then you can decide whom to vote for.

When you vote, you **make your voice heard**. That is one way to be a good citizen.

When Will I Be Old Enough to Vote?
People in the United States can and should vote when they turn eighteen.

Yes!
Your vote always counts.
Vote for the person you think would make the best class president.

You can talk to your classmates about your choice too. You can tell them why this person would be a good class president. You can even make posters. Explain your thoughts. Maybe they will vote with you!

VOTE!

You can wear your helmet. You can remember to signal your turns. Make sure to read and obey any road signs you pass. Always stay with the group and listen to adults. You will be setting a great example.

This girl is signaling a left turn. You can signal a right turn by holding out your left arm bent at the elbow or holding out your right arm.

A teacher reminded me to walk, not run, in the hallway. But it wasn't my teacher.

DO I HAVE TO OBEY TEACHERS I DON'T KNOW?

Yes!
Good citizens respect authority. One way to do that is to **obey those in charge**. That could include teachers, parents, and police officers.

14

Here are some other ways you can show you respect authority:

- Pay attention to any instructions from crossing guards on your way to school.

- Follow the rules on your school bus.

- Listen when your friends' parents ask you a question. Reply politely.

Sometimes the best thing to do is **walk away**. This sets a good example because it shows other kids you don't want to fight. It helps **keep the peace** in your school.

Tell an adult what happened. A teacher or a parent can help stop fights at school. Your school will be a safer place because of you.

My friend often makes fun of another kid at our bus stop. I know that's not the **right thing** to do. But it's hard to know when to walk away. **Do good citizens always walk away from conflict?**

No. You should not walk away if someone is hurting someone else. You should **speak up**. Tell your friend you don't agree with that kind of talk.

This sets a good example. It helps the person being teased. And it shows other kids the right way to behave.

Bullying is never okay. If you see someone being hurt, speak up or find an adult.

The lady who lives next door broke her leg. She has to be on crutches for a few weeks. CAN I BE A GOOD CITIZEN BY HELPING MY NEIGHBOR?

When you have a neighbor in need, you have a great chance to make a difference in your community. You can be a good citizen by helping out.

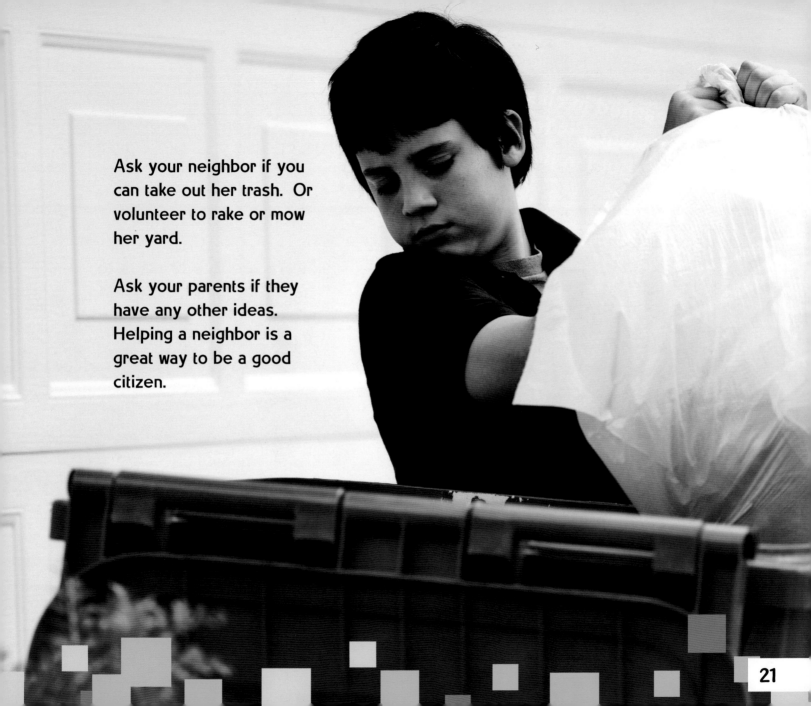

Ask your neighbor if you can take out her trash. Or volunteer to rake or mow her yard.

Ask your parents if they have any other ideas. Helping a neighbor is a great way to be a good citizen.

I learned in class how important it is to protect Earth. But I'm just one kid. **WHAT CAN I DO TO PROTECT OUR PLANET?**

There are lots of ways to help the planet. You can **recycle** glass, plastic, and paper. Ask your family to help you recycle.

You can volunteer to **pick up trash** in the park. You can even organize a cleanup day. Ask your friends to help you.

When you protect Earth, you are a good citizen.

Other Ways to Protect the Planet

Reusing things is a great way to protect Earth. Try using old boxes or shopping bags for craft projects. Get creative! You can also help save energy. Flip off the lights when you leave a room. Help your family remember to turn off the TV and the computer too.

Making less waste helps save the planet. Replace disposable water bottles with one reusable bottle.

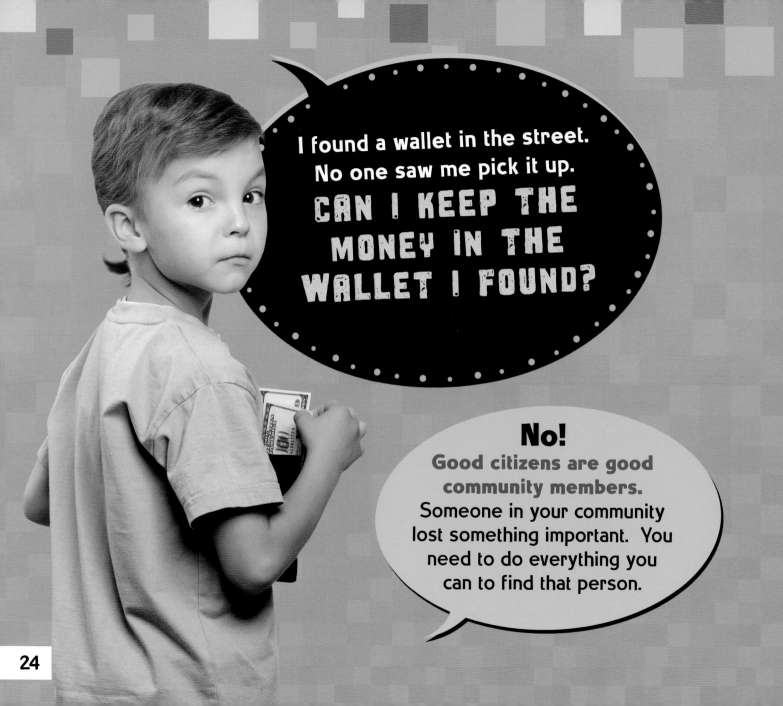

Look inside the wallet for a name. Can you tell whom the wallet belongs to? If so, you can return it. If not, you can ask the police to help find the owner. Bring the wallet to a police station. They will hold it in case someone asks about it. You can feel good. You know you did the right thing!

I want to help people who are really in need. I'd like to give them money. But I don't have much money of my own.

HOW CAN I HELP IF I DON'T HAVE MUCH MONEY?

There are lots of ways to help people. You don't need any money for most of the ways to help. You can **volunteer** in your community.

Try one of these ideas:

- Collect toys for kids who don't have any.

- Collect warm jackets or other useful items. Donate them to kids who need them.

- Help younger kids with reading or homework.

It's not hard to be a good citizen. You just have to think about others. Think about people in your school or community. Make choices that help everyone. Then you're being a good citizen!

Take this fun quiz to see how much you know about being a good citizen.

True or False?

1. You can't be a good citizen until you're old enough to vote.

2. Helping someone mow his or her lawn is one way to be a good citizen.

3. Good citizens squirt water guns at their neighbors on hot days.

4. Making fun of people who don't vote is part of being a good citizen.

5. Good citizens follow rules and obey authority.

6. Turning off the lights while your sister is reading makes you a good citizen.

7. Good citizens always tattle on other people.

8. You have to have a lot of money to be a good citizen.

9. You can be a good citizen even if you're not powerful.

10. People in the movies or on TV are all good citizens.

11. You can be a good citizen only during an election.

12. The best citizens always tell others what to do.

13. Yelling at the top of your lungs is the best way to make your voice heard.

14. One way to be a good citizen is to pick up trash.

15. Good citizens always walk away when they don't agree with what someone else is doing.

authority: the people who are in charge or have power

citizen: a person who has the right to do things such as work and vote in the country where he or she lives. A citizen can also be a person who lives in a certain community, town, or city.

conflict: a fight or disagreement

election: the process of choosing someone or deciding something by voting

obey: to do what someone tells you to do

recycle: to save old items such as glass, plastic, newspapers, and cans so they can be used to make new products

respect: consideration or courtesy. If you treat someone with respect, you treat him or her how you would like to be treated.

volunteer: to do a job without pay

Bailey, Jacqui. *What's the Point of Being Green?* Hauppauge, NY: Barron's Educational Series, 2010. Wondering how you can be a better citizen by protecting the planet? This book is full of helpful information and tips.

Citizenship
http://bensguide.gpo.gov/3-5/citizenship/index.html
"Ben's Guide to US Government for Kids" describes the rights and responsibilities of being a US citizen. It also provides information about becoming a US citizen.

Community Service
http://www.epa.gov/students/communityservice.html
Looking for a way to get involved in your community and help Earth too? This website from the US Environmental Protection Agency has lots of good ideas.

Donovan, Sandy. *When Is It My Turn? A Book about Fairness.* Minneapolis: Lerner Publications, 2014. Read about treating all people fairly in this book just for kids.

Nelson, Robin, and Sandy Donovan. *Getting Elected: A Look at Running for Office.* Minneapolis: Lerner Publications, 2012. Read all about elections and how US citizens elect people to public office.

PHOTO ACKNOWLEDGMENTS

The images in this book are used with the permission of: © Comstock Images, p. 4; © Biosphoto/ SuperStock, p. 5; © iStockphoto.com/SteveStone, p. 6; © iStockphoto.com/knape, p. 7; © Dirk Anschutz/ Stone/Getty Images, pp. 8, 10; © Richard Hutchings/CORBIS, p. 9; © iStockphoto.com/asiseeit, pp. 11, 27; © iStockphoto.com/Mark Bowden, p. 12; © Photononstop/SuperStock, p. 13; © Absodels/Getty Images, p. 14; © Blend Images/SuperStock, p. 15; © Relaximages/Getty Images, p. 16; © Monkey Business Images/ Shutterstock.com, p. 17; © Stefano Lunardi/Dreamstime.com, p. 18; © Inspirestock/Glow Images, p. 19; © The Welfare & Medical Care/Getty Images, p. 20; © iStockphoto.com/Juanmonino, p. 21; © Webbing1/ Dreamstime.com, p. 23; © DenisNata/Shutterstock.com, p. 24; © Huntstock-Fotolia.com, p. 25.

Front Cover: © Richard Hutchings/CORBIS.

Main body text set in ChurchwardSamoa Regular. Typeface provided by Chank.